Living in the Digital Age

A Christian Recipe for Authentic Human Development

by
Jean Pierre Casey

*All booklets are published thanks to the
generous support of the members of the
Catholic Truth Society*

CATHOLIC TRUTH SOCIETY
PUBLISHERS TO THE HOLY SEE

This paper was originally prepared at the request of the Foundation Centesimus Annus pro Pontifice. The author presented an abridged version at the 2017 Annual Conference of the Centesimus Annus pro Pontifice Foundation at the Vatican. The paper is circulated under the author's sole responsibility to elicit comments and to encourage debate; the views therein expressed are solely those of the author and do not necessarily represent the views of the CAPP Foundation or indeed of any institution with which the author may be affiliated. The author gratefully acknowledges comments made by Dr Adrian Pabst on an abridged version of this paper.

ISBN 978 1 78469 199 8

Contents

Introduction 5

1. Facts: What is happening
and what are the consequences? 8

1a. Spiritual and mental fragility arising
from the digital revolution 11

1b. Social fragility arising
from the digital revolution 15

1c. Economic fragility and civil liberty fragility
arising from the digital revolution 23

2. Principles: What does the Christian Social
Doctrine have to say about the development
and use of new [digital] technologies? 32

2a. The Church's nuanced position
vis-à-vis technical innovation 32

2b. Opportunities the Church sees
in the digital revolution. 41

2c. Threats the Church sees
from the digital revolution 45

2d. Christian Social Doctrine principles:
application to the development,
distribution and use of digital technologies 49

**3. Action: How can the Christian Social Doctrine
guide the laity to help them engage with technology
companies and inform the public debate?** 56

Bibliography of sources drawn
from the Christian Social Doctrine 60

Endnotes 63

Introduction

In terms of the breadth and depth of its impact, the *digital revolution* and all that came with it – the facilitation and acceleration of *access*, broadly writ, through the internet and connected devices; the ability to track and capture records of billions of users' online activity; the digitalisation and dematerialisation of commerce; the rise of social networking; machine learning and the advent of artificial intelligence – is no doubt one of the most disruptive technological shifts in the history of humankind. Unlike great innovations that propelled humankind to greater heights, whether in the fields of medicine, engineering, agronomy, or physics – the internet, combined with advances in computational powers, has also profoundly affected and indeed altered, human behaviours, particularly in the way we interact. This difference is what makes the disruptive nature of digital technology particularly interesting to study from a Christian lens, as the Social Doctrine of the Church aims to assess the essence of such developments from the holistic perspective of the common good, going right to the core of what it means to be human, and not just uncritically from the unidimensional perspective of 'progress'.

It is precisely because the penetration of digital technology – via connected devices and the 'internet of things' – runs so deep into the economy, into our daily lives, and into spheres of social interaction; and because its ability to manipulate, control and distort is so complete, that the digital revolution, also known as the fourth industrial revolution, requires a specifically Christian response.

There is a need for urgency, since "humanity today is at a crossroads," as Pope Benedict XVI puts it, owing to the speed at which these technologies have been introduced and are evolving. In many ways, we have been caught unawares by the wholesale changes wrought by the digital revolution: our economic, political and legal frameworks have not sufficiently evolved to address its undeniably significant cross-cutting impacts. The scale and scope of spiritual and mental ailments associated with high rates of digital penetration also demonstrate that collectively, the People of God have been poorly equipped spiritually and pastorally to deal with these challenges, including being deficient in the collective cultivation of moral fortitude that is requisite in the digital era.

This contribution aims to formulate a specifically Christian response to the manifold challenges the digital era presents, by:

1. highlighting the accelerating nature of change the digital revolution has introduced; and analysing the challenges these innovations present from the spiritual, socio-anthropological and economic perspectives;

2. reviewing the principles of the Christian Social Doctrine that can be applied to address specific issues and reminding the readership of the richness and breadth of the Church's teaching with regard to technological breakthroughs, including digital;

3. offering some suggestions on what constitutes an ordered use of these new digital technologies according to the Christian Social Doctrine and on how the lay Christian community can be informed, engaged, responsible, courageous and holy actors in the digital era.

1. Facts: What is happening and what are the consequences?

The pervasiveness of the digital revolution is not to be underestimated, hence why the Pontifical Council for Culture has also dubbed it a "cultural revolution", why Pope Benedict described it as a "period of vast cultural transformation" and why, more recently, Pope Francis has spoken of the "cultural crisis of our time" at the Plenary Assembly of the Pontifical Council for the Laity in 2013, whose theme was "Announcing Christ in the Digital Age". Major providers of internet or cloud services expect an explosion in connected devices over the next three years. Intel expects some two hundred billion to be in circulation by 2020, an average of more than twenty per person on the planet. In the West, time spent on connected devices is enormous – ten hours average per day for Americans and nearly nine hours per day for Britons, which exceeds the number of hours of sleep for the average person. The average person logs into their iPhones eighty times per day. The 'internet of things' has an insatiable appetite to digitise virtually everything. 'Smart' devices are being implanted in everything from household appliances to machinery to motor vehicles, and possibly into humans as well, in the near future (live pilot tests are already underway). The rapid progress of artificial intelligence and robotics is fundamentally changing the way we use and interact with previously inanimate objects.

These changes have immense consequences for the spiritual life, for family life, for social ties and socio-economic organisation, not to mention for the "formation of personality and conscience, the interpretation and structuring of affective relationships, the coming together of the educative and formative phases, [and] the elaboration and diffusion of cultural phenomena."[1] With such dramatic shifts in lifestyle, in the forms of economic organisation and the ecosystem of social structures, we need to take stock of what have we gained, *vs* what have we lost, with the advent of the internet. Thus, it is legitimate to ask: what have been the fruits of these new technologies? Have they drawn us closer to God? Have they helped us to better express our solidarity with others? Have they enriched us culturally and spiritually? Have they allowed us to better express our respective vocations and to develop our human potential? Without being overly pessimistic, and whilst acknowledging the many positive characteristics of digital applications, the answer to many of these questions is, unfortunately, no.

Despite the great potential of digital applications to be used for good, it is evident, after twenty five or so years, that they have contributed to tremendous fragility in our societies: spiritual and mental fragility, social fragility, economic fragility, and civil liberty fragility, heretofore unquestioned.

1a. Spiritual and mental fragility arising from the digital revolution

The culture of instant gratification accentuated by constant digital connectivity has created immense spiritual and mental fragility. One consequence is that metaphysical concepts such as sin, which are inherently tied to incarnate beings, are challenged, or at a very minimum need to be re-explained, in light of the development of a parallel virtual universe alongside the physical universe. Another consequence is that we are constantly looking for stimulation in the digital era. This perpetual state of agitation is eating away at that sacred space in the soul where the Holy Spirit whispers. We have lost the virtue of patience, as the ability to instantly gratify our needs through a "click and buy" mentality has intensified the lust for consumerism and other base instincts. Our days can now be summarised as a sequence of one type of impulsive movement, clicking or swiping. In stark contrast to such mindless activity is the Christian view of meaningfulness, as defined by Pope Benedict XVI: "Life is not just a succession of events and experiences: it is a search for the true, the good and the beautiful."[2]

Thus, our era is marked by a struggle with a new problem, the addiction to 'sensoriousness'. We live under siege, constantly bombarded by sensory signals, which Cardinal Sarah has qualified the "dictatorship of noise". These signals disrupt our minds and souls, constantly distract us from our thought processes, from productive economic, social, cultural and humanitarian activity, from praying, and from spending quality time with our loved ones. Pope Francis has explicitly alluded to this problem in his Apostolic Exhortation *Amoris Laetitia* (278): "We know that sometimes [these media devices] can keep people apart rather than together, as when at dinnertime everyone is surfing on a mobile phone, or when one spouse falls asleep waiting for the other who spends hours playing with an electronic device." Making an ordered use of digitally connected devices is especially problematic for the (vulnerable) younger generations who grew up with these technologies as toddlers, whom Pope Benedict XVI has described as the "digital generation" and for whom the web is "connatural" according to Pope Francis, almost as if it were an extension of their beings. Passively consuming or producing large volumes of digital data in a compulsive manner has led to the carving out of the animus, that combination of soul and mind. To give an indication of the scale of the problem and the sheer volume of information produced, consider these numbers. Every single minute of the day: users 'like' over four million Facebook posts;

YouTube users upload over three hundred hours of video; Apple users download over fifty five thousand apps; Amazon's website receives over four thousand visitors; Instagram users 'like' over 1.7 million photos; Twitter users send nearly three hundred and fifty thousand tweets; Snapchat users share almost three hundred thousand snaps.

This constant quest for sensory stimulation and addiction to screens makes us less productive, less interior, less focused, less capable of critical thinking, and less attentive to the needs of others, as mental health issues like narcissism and compulsive/pathological internet use become ever more widespread. The era of the selfie has produced a generation of narcissists, and the numbers are telling: Anil Sabharwal, Vice President of Google Photos, the eponymous search engine's digital photography warehouse, wrote in a blog on Google's website that the two hundred million users of Google Photos uploaded twenty four billion selfies in the first year of operations, meaning an average of about one hundred per year per user, or about one every three to four days. Previously thought to have been purely hypothetical concerns, both narcissism and compulsive/pathological internet use are now recognised as mass clinical phenomena by mental health practitioners like neuroscientists and psychologists, by authoritative scientific bodies, and even by medical doctors, given the proven adverse consequences these psychosocial conditions have not only on mental health, but also on physical well-being, not least of which are the morphological changes to the brain observed in internet addicts, with their seemingly insatiable appetite for external stimuli.

Other negative physiological effects like deteriorating immunological, cardiovascular and neuroendocrine functioning have all been found in intra-sample subsets of observed populations who tend to interact virtually via digital channels proportionally more than those whose social interactions occur more frequently in the physical world. As for the mental health consequences of digital addiction, "sleep deprivation, academic under-achievement, failure to exercise and to engage in face-to-face social activities, negative affective states, and decreased ability to concentrate were frequently reported consequences of intensive internet use/internet overuse," according to a recent scientific study. Like other forms of addiction, digital addiction has also been linked to loss of appetite and enhanced anxiety. Thus, the neurobiological effects of digital addiction have been found to be very similar to those of opiates. This scientific finding has been recognised by the Church (more specifically by the Pontifical Council for Communications in its text *Ethics in Communications*): "Depending on how they use media, people can grow in sympathy and compassion or become isolated in a narcissistic, self-referential world of stimuli with *near-narcotic effects*" (emphasis added).[3]

1b. Social fragility arising from the digital revolution

Virtual culture has also led to a deconstruction of the very fabric of society, leading to enhanced social fragility, reflected in symptoms associated with a culture of radical individualism like increasing loneliness and isolation; a general apathy towards and disengagement from community life such as involvement in the political process, volunteering, religious worship, membership in clubs and groups of various natures; the acceleration of the breakdown of marriage and other established forms of inter-personal relationships; and in the general sense of helplessness, disorientation and resignation/fatalism arising from our increasing inability to distinguish between the real and virtual worlds, as they collide, and even merge, at a frightening pace.

The increasing social isolation of individuals who are 'too connected' digitally is a recognised phenomenon. Sentiments of loneliness and depression are far more likely to be expressed by those who spend more, rather than less, time on their connected devices. Scientific studies have found causal linkages between increased social media use and depression. Importantly, there is documented evidence pointing to a causal link between social isolation and declining physical well-being. Victims of social isolation are more accident prone, are at greater risk of developing psychiatric disorders and face a greater risk of early mortality.

The social cost of the misuse of digital technology is not just limited to the mental and physical health issues aggravated in the digital era. Victims of these conditions may also suffer lifelong adverse economic effects as their productivity and employability is sapped by their inability to concentrate due to the sharp reduction in attention spans: higher incidence rates of attention deficit disorder (ADD) and hyperactivity disorder (ADHD) have also been observed among digital addicts, alongside depression.

In a digital world, the worst kinds of temptations are only a click or a swipe away. Pornography has reached epidemic proportions and is considered, rightly, in some countries as a public health crisis. Between half and two-thirds of American men, and over thirty per cent of women report porn use over a given year, according to a recent study comparing the results of four different nationally representative samples in the United States. Pornography accounts for a large proportion of total web content and searches, and has exceptionally serious consequences for family life and personal well-being, despite the popular view, often supported by liberal media outlets, that it is "harmless" because it only involves virtual fantasies. This naïve view completely ignores the real life consequences of porn use, such as its correlation with social ineptness like withdrawal symptoms, not to mention its undeniable causal link to divorce, via marriage and family breakdown, as well as a clear association with violent crimes like sexual assault (which suggests that there is some truth to the feminist dictum that "pornography is the theory – rape is the practice").

Some statistics on the epidemic proportions of online pornography are given by *The Week* periodical, citing as sources, among others, CNBC, *The Washington Times*, and *The Huffington Post*: one hundred billion dollars of pornography sales globally, annually; seven out of ten children inadvertently see pornographic content online; eleven is the average age at which a child first encounters pornographic content; nearly thirty thousand internet users are viewing pornography, every second; twenty five per cent of all internet-based searches are pornography related; twelve per cent of all websites contain pornographic material; nearly three hundred new pornography websites are developed every day, meaning over one hundred thousand new porn websites come online every year. The reach of pornography has only intensified with the proliferation of handheld electronic devices like smartphones, tablets and the like. It doesn't stop there.

The 'pornographication' of our culture marches on relentlessly, aided by these handheld electronic devices through which various apps facilitate casual sexual encounters, and even overtly promote marital infidelity. The epidemic is of biblical proportions; hardly a home is unaffected by it. Like a cancer, this tsunami of hidden perversion is secretly ravaging homes, families, souls and lives, despite the appearance of 'all being well' on the surface, behind the shiny facade of smiling children, physically fit spouses and 'healthy' diets. That software programmers are deliberately appealing to baser human instincts and preying on human vulnerability to drive their profits says something about the shape of the modern digital economy.

In light of these numerous ills, it is legitimate to question whether the contemporary addiction to sensoriousness is one which the developers of these gadgets, platforms, devices and apps are truly interested in resolving. Currently, the developers and operators of digital media platforms do not have any economic incentive to address the problem of digital addiction. The vulnerability of those suffering from digital addiction may derive in part from the fact that "social networks are…nourished by aspirations rooted in the human heart,"[4] as Pope Benedict XVI puts it. If anything, these networks aim to maximise the time users spend in the 'walled garden' of their closed digital circuit – whether an app or a website or an operating platform – in order to capture future revenue streams through various product enhancements or advertising revenues tied to the intensity, longevity and/or ubiquity of user activity. Ironically, many Silicon Valley bosses send their children to tech-free or digitally sanitised schools, which leads one to question the social and educational utility of the digital products their firms are developing. All of this points to the necessity of developing strong ethical guidelines, and/or an accompanying regulatory framework, which is why the input of laypersons formed by the Christian Social Doctrine is so vital in these debates.

Social fragility is further magnified in the digital era through the blending of the virtual and physical worlds. Indeed, this is the dream of some in Silicon Valley: to make digital not only a reflection of the real, but indeed an extension of the real, and furthermore, to make virtual reality the new 'reality', thereby "blurring the distinction between truth and illusion", as Pope St John Paul II prophetically warned. Whereas once they were nothing but the fanciful dreams of science fiction enthusiasts, developments such as uploading the human brain onto servers; enhancing cognitive abilities via the merger of biological and artificial intelligence (AI); augmenting sensory or physical prowess through the welding of mechanised body parts onto biological bodies, whether those parts be AI-driven autonomous extensions, or digitally connected to the physical body's neurological system so as to follow impulses generated by a human brain as opposed to by AI – is the reality of scientific exploration in our generation. Some of those close to the action plead for transhumanist enhancements merely for the human species to 'remain relevant' or even as a question of survival for humans in a world where we will co-exist alongside autonomous, artificially intelligent 'beings' whose machine-learning abilities will allow them to act as if they had a mind of their own.

The urge to press ahead in the name of 'progress' is so great, and advances in artificial intelligence are so rapid, that we hardly have time to consider, let alone organise, adequate public policy debates on the most basic metaphysical, philosophical, legal and political questions associated with these developments, at a time when tech leaders have already been talking about a 'post-human' world for some time: what happens to the nature of man in this convergence of the natural world and virtual reality? What are the consequences spiritually or otherwise for the blending of the virtual and the real? What does it mean for our ability to marvel at God's creation as we spend more and more time as prisoners in the virtual worlds we have created? What does the virtualisation of man, living in a parallel universe which is not reality, mean for his psyche, for his soul, for his human relations, for his development, for his happiness, for his good? The quest for man's search for meaning can only be satisfied in divine revelation, through the person of Jesus Christ, as explained by Pope St John Paul II: "the glorious truth about human life and human destiny [is] revealed in the Word *made flesh*" (emphasis added). The Christian religion is the religion of the Incarnate Word, by virtue of the miracle of the Emmanuel, 'God with us', in the person of Jesus Christ. Beyond the specific historical event of the Incarnation, and owing to the Incarnation, Christianity is the religion of incarnation, more broadly defined, which means embodiment in the flesh, i.e. the celebration of a material, living substance. Virtual reality is the antithesis of incarnation. It is an alternative to the natural, physical world, created by God. It is therefore a caricature of reality, an artifice, and therefore an illusion, a deception. Because it is the antithesis of incarnation, it is, by definition, anti-Christian.

So what does the blending of the natural reality of human existence with 'augmented' reality characteristics – as the transhumanist movement aims to pioneer – mean for the very nature of humankind and for the future of mankind? How will robots with artificial intelligence (AI) co-exist with, or possibly compete, with humans (and not just in the work environment)? How will these cyber-conscious beings be recognised in legal frameworks – will they be given legal personality? How will 'transhuman' beings with AI-augmented physical and intellectual capabilities compete for work with 'natural' humans who are not AI-augmented? How will human rights frameworks be adapted or not to recognise the difference between these different classes of human? Why are we so keen on developing machine-augmentation of human faculties? To what end? What risks are there that advances in transhumanism will lead to a digital divide within the physical essence of humans, separating those with machine-augmented faculties from those who wish to preserve the integrity of their unenhanced natural biological bodies or who do not have the financial means to 'upgrade' their humanity to cyborg status? To what extent will the transhumanist movement lead to an instrumentalisation of man by converting people into machines through enhanced cognitive and sensory capabilities, heightened physical strength and a slowing of the ageing process? The consequences of our collective loss of connection with reality, of our loss of connection with nature, the consequences of losing our willingness and/or ability to reflect adequately on the desirability of some of these outcomes is not to be underestimated.

Despite the grave consequences for the future of humanity these critical normative questions raise with ever greater urgency as these developments accelerate, there remains an astounding silence on the part of the Church, of political leaders and of civil society. The need for Christians and all people of good will to inform themselves, engage in the political process and influence these worrisome trends cannot be underestimated. Indeed, the question of the very substance of our humanity, the "anthropological question," as Pope Benedict XVI puts it, is the "key challenge of the third millennium."

1c. Economic fragility and civil liberty fragility arising from the digital revolution

The emergence of the 'internet of things' and 'smart' technology being implanted in everything from household appliances like refrigerators and boilers to cars to heavy industrial machinery means that basic manufactured goods being sold are nothing more than digital devices with handy secondary applications like motorised movement or temperature control. Mass digital connectivity to the internet via 'smart' devices contributes materially to enhanced economic fragility and to the fragility of civil liberties. That so little public policy discussion has been undertaken to address the extreme vulnerability such inter-connectedness introduces into the economy and into society – where unwanted intrusion via household electronic circuitry into the electricity grid, into financial markets trading platforms, and into military installations could have almost apocalyptic consequences – is symptomatic of the unquestioning euphoria accompanying the fourth industrial revolution.

With regard to fundamental freedoms, an undeniable consequence of participating in the cyber universe is suffering a lack of privacy as never before experienced in the history of man, to such an extent that it is not an exaggeration to speak of the death of privacy. Millions of surveillance cameras across the world, not to mention an increasing number of digital applications and wired devices, operate facial recognition technology. The physical movements of any member of the population are now being tracked in almost the same way as if we were felons wearing electronic monitoring bracelets. All internet users globally, throughout all time, have a permanently indelible 'digital footprint' giving governments the ability to track absolutely everything anyone has ever clicked on, typed, downloaded or uploaded from or to the internet. Thus, an unintended consequence, or perhaps a deliberate purpose of, the digital revolution has been to generate what *The Guardian* newspaper has called "the greatest mass surveillance infrastructure ever."

That the tentacles of the internet are reaching deeper and deeper into the lives of individuals through the spontaneous or forced adoption of the 'internet of things' (for example, the UK government wants "energy suppliers to install 'smart meters' in every home in England, Wales and Scotland by 2020"), means that inanimate objects suddenly become 'animate'. That is, they can be used, and will be used, to spy on the activities of the masses by relaying information on the conversations, movements, and purchases of average citizens to external agents unknown to them, and often without their knowledge or consent. As noted by the US Director of National Intelligence James Clapper in a 2016 testimony before the United States Congress, "in the future, intelligence services might use the [internet of things] for identification, surveillance, monitoring, location tracking and targeting for recruitment, or to gain access to networks or user credentials."

Finally, the widespread dissemination of digital devices has enhanced the ability of certain powers – and not just non-state actors like the media, extremist groups or those driven by particular ideologies – to manipulate, censor and distort information, as well as to misinform, on an unprecedented scale in history, because nowadays, Pope Benedict XVI says, "search engines and social networks have become the starting point of communication for many people who are seeking advice, ideas, information and answers."[5] More specifically, the Pontifical Council for Social Communications has warned of the ability of the communications media to "be vehicles [propagating] a deformed outlook on life, on the family, on religion and on morality." This ability to distort and influence news, data, and societal values, and to channel controversial messaging to minors without the knowledge or consent of their parents is highly problematic according to Pope St John Paul II, to the extent that "communications media have acquired such importance as to be the principal means of guidance and inspiration for many people in their personal, familial and social behaviour." He also understood that communication via digital media increasingly "influences the consciences of individuals, form[s] their mentality and determine[s] their view of things."

The manipulation of digital information can take numerous forms. It ranges from the publication and diffusion of fake news and hyped news to treating news as entertainment, as news agencies move from reporting news to "creating news", considered by Pope Benedict XVI to be a "dangerous change in function;" to the ability to influence or radicalise from afar, outside of the established legal framework of particular jurisdictions, giving rise to the risk that lawless parallel societies spawn within countries supposedly governed by the rule of law; to mass censorship through 'big data' mining techniques screening millions of social media posts, blogs and websites, in order to withdraw from digital circulation any information deemed undesirable for any multitude of reasons.

In the wake of numerous recent terrorist attacks, digital platform operators are increasingly under pressure from governments to censor extremist online material that can be considered to incite violence. However, in the absence of a proper, internationally-recognised legal definition of 'extremist' content, there is a real risk that non-state actors with various ideological agendas are already pressuring digital network operators and internet search/service providers to use their newfound censoring powers to remove from internet search engine results or from social media feeds any public or private messaging with which they disagree. This untransparent lobbying for censorship of subjectively offensive online content has the potential to turn into a direct assault on the most fundamental freedoms that have been the pillars of the western democratic system, such as the freedoms of religion, expression and association. One can easily imagine a scenario where social media operators remove the ability of certain individuals or groups to generate ad revenues from their pages, or to post ads, or to curate, post and distribute online content, or even to access online content, on the basis that their messaging is offensive or inappropriate – determined on a purely subjective or emotional, as opposed to legitimate legal, basis. Indeed, the increasing politicisation of western corporations has already led to active 'thought police' surveillance and sanction tactics in both the public and private digital communication spheres.

What will these newfound censorship powers mean in the 'politically correct' era where Christian values, or more broadly, religious values, are systematically being eradicated from the public arena, and when there is not only increasing intolerance, but even outright hostility towards, any views that do not correspond to the prevailing "dictatorship of relativism", a condition in which, according to Pope St John Paul II, the "only absolute truth is that there are no absolute truths"? What does it mean for religious freedom? What does it mean for the freedom of speech? For the freedom of association? For press freedom? For the freedom of movement? Who will determine whether or not online content is deemed 'appropriate', 'suitable', 'not offensive', 'safe', 'inclusive', or 'offensive'? How will that determination be made? By whom? With what controls or safeguards? With what levels of transparency around the criteria of selection or process to be followed, around how those criteria were arrived at and on who influenced them? Neither blind, unquestioning acceptance of these tendencies nor a resigned fatalism are an adequate posture to adopt in the face of these threats.

***

The digitalisation of the economy and increased automation of productive processes has also led to intensified economic fragility. One good example would be the increasing fragility of infrastructures, i.e. their lack of robustness or resilience in the face of an exogenous shock – whether power networks or financial markets or supply chains – through digital interconnectivity, which leads to spill-over effects previously not possible in a more diverse infrastructural ecosystem.

Another good example is the anticipation that worker displacement will only accelerate with the rapid advance of robotics. What began with automation in the manufacturing sector now threatens to extend much more broadly, as whole sectors of the economy are rapidly being "digitally mechanised", removing any need for human workers, whether cashiers, taxi/bus/truck drivers, factory workers, hospitality sector workers including, but not limited to, cleaners and packagers/sorters. In the words of former US Treasury Secretary Lawrence Summers, "this isn't some hypothetical future possibility – this is something that's emerging before us right now." In the not-too-distant future, worker displacement via smart technology will extend to higher skilled professions like administrative and research roles, pilots, security/military personnel and some medical jobs. Indeed, a number of economists and business leaders expect worker displacement by robots with artificial intelligence to be unprecedented in its speed and scale over the coming decade, with huge consequences for the economic welfare and mental health of workers. A general state of unpreparedness for a labour market shock of this magnitude could lead to unintended consequences like large-scale civil unrest and the rise of extremist political parties.

Academics, pundits, political scientists and business leaders are openly talking of the advent of the post-work era, which was already predicted by famous British economist John Maynard Keynes in 1930 when he suggested a fifteen-hour working week to resolve the problem of finite human consumption versus the seemingly inexorable march of technical innovation combined with the perpetual accumulation of capital. Today, the CEO and co-founder of Google is advocating openly a variation of Keynes' policy prescription to solve the employment dilemma by proposing the adoption of a government-imposed shortening of the working week.

***

Having reviewed some of the consequences of all these technological advances in the digital sphere, the main question from a Christian point of view is: have they contributed positively to *authentic* or *integral* human development? The broad categories of spiritual, social and economic ailments deriving from the digital revolution are the clearest sign that something is not right, either with the nature of some of these digital technologies, or with their use, or both. Taking stock in a dispassionate manner of these adverse consequences deriving from the creation of digital applications is a specific Christian calling, as "the Church has always had the duty of scrutinising the signs of the times and of interpreting them in the light of the gospel."[6] These different categories of ailments are undeniably the signs of our times, as this paper argues, supported by a multidisciplinary review of peer-reviewed research and credible pieces published by authoritative news organisations.

It is against this admittedly bleak backdrop of, paradoxically, an enhanced human vulnerability in the digital era – which in our view has not been sufficiently scrutinised, owing to the fact that the spiritual, social and economic costs of digital technology are often hidden, lurking under the surface in corrupted souls, broken homes, weakened minds – that we would like to propose a menu of policy, behavioural and spiritual responses, inspired from the Christian Social Doctrine, to provide a framework for a healthy usage of these new digital technologies in an ordered way.

2. Principles: What does the Christian Social Doctrine have to say about the development and use of new [digital] technologies?

2a. The Church's nuanced position *vis-à-vis* technical innovation

In line with her general message of hope, the Church's position with regard to new technologies is for the most part nuanced, and could be characterised as 'cautiously optimistic'. As an "expert in humanity" the Church is naturally cautious, because she is all too aware of the human proclivity to sin. Pope Benedict XVI, for example, speaks of the "extraordinary potential" of the media following their "meteoric technological evolution," but he also warns of "hitherto unimaginable questions and problems" associated with their genesis. Caution is not only warranted because of human failings, but also because in the face of rapid technological progress like the digital revolution, its "full implications are as yet imperfectly understood," as Pope St John Paul II wrote in one of his World Communications Day's addresses, *The Christian Message in a Computer Culture*.

The Church generally recognises the "ambiguity of progress" (e.g. in Pope Benedict XVI's Encyclical Letter *Spe Salvi*) and the *moral neutrality* of technological innovations, so long as proper use is made of them, as "these are not blind forces of nature beyond human control," as the Pontifical Council for Social Communications reminds us. From a moral theology point of view, it is critically important to distinguish between the potential moral neutrality of the technology behind contemporary communications channels, and the morality of the use made of them by humans participating in the act of communication. Whereas the moral neutrality of the communications devices themselves is a position generally held by the Church subject to certain conditions, their use is not beyond the moral order, because human communication is, by definition, a "moral act" according to Pope St John Paul II, quoting St Matthew 12:35-37. Indeed, Pope Francis notes that "it is not technology which determines whether or not communication is authentic, but rather the human heart and our capacity to use wisely the means at our disposal."[7]

Recognising the positive effects of new forms of communication made possible by technological progress, the Church has gone even so far as to call them a "gift from God" (Pope Pius XII in his 1957 Encyclical Letter *Miranda Prorsus*, and Pope Francis in his 2014 Message for the 48th World Communications Day, *Communication*

at the Service of an Authentic Culture of Encounter).
Computers, the internet and other instruments facilitating
digital communication are a "gift for humanity"
(Pope Benedict XVI in his 2009 Message for the 43rd
World Communications Day, *New Technologies, New
Relationships. Promoting a Culture of Respect, Dialogue
and Friendship*), for which we must be "grateful" (Pope
St John Paul II in his 1990 Message for the 24th World
Communications Day, *The Christian Message in a
Computer Culture*). The Church speaks of these new
communication technologies as "marvellous technical
inventions" (Pope St John Paul II in his 2005 Apostolic
Letter *The Rapid Development*) or indeed *Inter Mirifica*,
"among the wonderful" (Bl. Pope Paul VI in his eponymous
1963 Decree on the Media of Social Communications).
Because of the opportunities it offers for "encounter
and solidarity," the internet is something "truly good"
(Pope Francis in his 2014 Message for the 48th World
Communications Day, *Communication at the Service of
an Authentic Culture of Encounter*). All of this suggests
the Church's position vis-à-vis these technologies goes
beyond considering them to be merely morally neutral. On
the contrary, the teachings of recent popes suggests that
the Church almost considers these digital technologies to
be an absolute moral 'good' – a good, which like all fruits
of creation or derivatives thereof developed by virtue of
man's intelligence, must be orientated towards the true,

the good and the beautiful, all of which are summarised in the person of Jesus Christ. It is therefore incumbent upon Christians to make "creative use of the new discoveries and technologies for the benefit of humanity and the fulfilment of God's plan for the world."[8] Pope St John Paul II specifically admonishes us to refrain from being afraid of them, in his Apostolic Letter *The Rapid Development*.

Despite highlighting the positive characteristics of certain innovations, including digital devices, the Church also recognises the dangers that certain technologies or their disordered use can present for the common good. Our constant quest for progress is symptomatic of a kind of messianic humanism where man, making a false god of human reasoning, believes he is the sole master of his own destiny and can solve all the world's ills, to the extent of replacing the City of God with the Temple of Man. The Church explicitly denounces the intra-worldly ideology of progress as "contrary to the integral truth of the human person and to God's plan in history."[9] This disordered quest to engineer his own temporal, as opposed to eternal, salvation pushes man, under the pretext of 'humanism' and 'progress', to experiment ever further, without proper discernment or prayer.

Scientific progress has accelerated to such an extent in recent years that without strong ethical principles and a robust regulatory framework, the explosive cocktail of genetics, life sciences, robotics and digital technologies can be said to threaten the very substance of the human species. Pope Benedict XVI cautions in his Encyclical Letter *Spe Salvi* that certain forms of technological innovation can "open…up appalling possibilities for evil that formerly did not exist."

Thus, human dignity becomes secondary, and indeed almost considered an obstacle, to the messianic objective of achieving linear scientific progress over time. Believing that everything that is technically feasible is licit is a materialistic and utilitarian ideology that has been condemned numerous times by the Church, not least by Pope Benedict XVI: "not everything that is technically possible is also ethically permissible." Pope Francis warns in *Laudato Si* (136) that "when technology disregards the great ethical principles, it ends up considering any practice whatsoever as licit… A technology severed from ethics will not easily be able to limit its own power."

The ideology of progress has tempted man from the earliest days of creation. It first arose from the false enlightenment experienced by Adam and Eve, when, (mis-) guided by their reason, they betrayed their own consciences and the second commandment of their Creator. Original sin often clouds our judgement and hardens our hearts as their descendants, and our development of new technologies is no exception. New technologies are not always morally neutral, especially if they have been deliberately designed to engineer evil outcomes, or if the way they have evolved leads to the seduction, manipulation or corruption of the human mind and soul, or indeed if their primary purpose is to perpetuate injustice and suppress the vulnerable. Pope Francis has qualified misuse of digital technology as a "hindrance" and even as a form of "aggression." The Church is very much aware of these dangers, and her teachings are clear in warning us of the "new violations of human dignity and rights" that new technical capabilities can introduce.

Despite these dangers, the Church is not recommending a wholesale or even partial withdrawal from the digital universe. On the contrary, Pope Francis explicitly calls for us to "boldly become citizens of the digital world," stating that the drawbacks and potential evil uses of these applications "do not justify rejecting social media," not least because "the digital highway is…a street teeming with people who are often hurting, men and women looking for salvation or hope." The Church's doors must remain open to people who have lost hope, and meaning, and love, and faith, but they also need to be kept "open in the digital space." Neither are inanimate digital networks seen as the nemesis, because "it is not technology which determines whether or not communication is authentic, but rather the human heart and our capacity to use wisely the means at our disposal."[10] Furthermore, "the digital world can be an environment rich in humanity; a network not of wires but of people."[11]

The Church's nuanced view on technological developments, including digital applications, derives not only from the careful consideration she has given to these matters, but is a natural by-product of the wisdom with which she is endowed by the grace of the Holy Spirit as the Bride of Christ; of her natural intelligence as an "expert in humanity" and as an apologist for human dignity; of her extensive pastoral experience; and of her presence "in the very midst of human progress, sharing the experiences of the rest of humanity, seeking to understand them and to interpret them in the light of faith."[12] Boasting these unique qualities, the Church has not only the right but also the duty to opine on these matters, given that more advanced technologies amplify the consequences of moral choices. The digital revolution is no exception: "Great good or great evil come from the use people make of the media of social communication."[13]

So what constitutes "progress" from a Christian perspective and how are we meant to discern? Unlike in the scientific world, any advance in mechanical, computational or scientific prowess is clearly not a sufficient condition for progress, and perhaps not even a necessary condition. In his Encyclical *Redemptor Hominis*, John Paul II brought to life the abstract concept of the 'common good' with regard to technological progress by offering a compelling litmus test: are these new technical abilities leading the human person to "becom[e] truly better, that is to say more mature spiritually, more aware of the dignity of his humanity, more responsible, more open to others, especially the neediest and weakest, and readier to give and to aid all?"[14] This litmus test is but one instrument in the rich toolkit of resources the Church puts at our disposal to be informed, engaged, responsible, courageous and holy actors in the digital era.

Importantly, the Church does not view herself as an outsider to these developments, but rather as an important and active participant, who can help to influence the ordered use of new technologies. To this end, Pope Francis has considered the Church's online presence [to be] "indispensable," Pope St John Paul II admonished that the Church "cannot fail to be ever more deeply involved in the burgeoning world of communications" and the Pontifical Council for Social Communications suggests that "hanging back timidly from fear of technology…is not acceptable." Rather than fighting a rear-guard battle against technology and condemning it as evil, from the time of the chariot through to ships, the printing press, rocket science and now the digital revolution, the Church has always seized opportunities to use human innovations to preach the gospel, as expressed in the conciliar document *Gaudium et Spes*. This will explain why, despite the evident spiritual dangers that are associated with the digital revolution, the Church will "avail herself of…computer and satellite technology" and recognises the "ever new and far-reaching pastoral opportunities" it offers.

In the next section, we have tried to summarise the Church's nuanced view of digital advances as a catalogue of opportunities and risks, by piecing together a mosaic of different teachings collected from her vast Magisterium.

2b. Opportunities the Church sees in the digital revolution

- **Evangelisation** – the core mission of the Church is to make known to all nations the mystery of our creation and salvation: the unconditional love of God the Father that inspired him to create man and woman in his image and likeness, and the fulfilment of that promise of love through the incarnation, Passion and Resurrection of our Saviour Jesus Christ. Indeed, "the proclamation of the gospel…[is] the most important [possibility] offer[ed]…[by] digital communication"[15] and therefore ought to be considered, from a Christian perspective, its primary purpose. New means of communication made possible by technological advances can be a powerful instrument of evangelisation, as they provide "unprecedented opportunities for making the truth more accessible to many more people"[16] and allow us to "discover precious opportunities for leading men and women to the luminous Face of the Lord, …guided by the Holy Spirit."[17] Pope Benedict XVI uses poetic imagery to describe how the internet can help to be a vehicle channelling the Good News: "In this way the Word can traverse the many crossroads created by the intersection of all the different 'highways' that form 'cyberspace'".[18] The Church is "always... in search of new ways to proclaim the gospel,"[19] and digital media are just another instrument that can be effectively marshalled towards this end – a "powerful" means which she would "feel guilty before the Lord if she did not utilise."[20] Indeed, Pope St John Paul II considered the use of the "techniques and technologies of contemporary communications [as] an integral part of [the Church's] mission in the third millennium,"[21] as the new evangelisation requires the "enculturation of the gospel," obviously meant to include the digital realm.

- **Solidarity and growing in unity** – new channels of communication made possible by digital technology can "creat[e] a sense of unity of the human family which can in turn inspire solidarity and serious efforts to ensure a more dignified life for all."[22] Pope Benedict XVI speaks of their ability to "promote harmony." They can be "vehicles for...solidarity and peace," enabling a "real dialogue between widely-separated peoples, ...a worldwide sharing of ideas and aspirations, ...a strengthening of brotherhood across many hitherto insurmountable barriers."[23] These digital innovations can also be a means for us to "encounter...real women and men, who are often wounded or lost, in order to give them real reasons to hope."[24]

- **Advancing the Church's mission by supporting her in her government and her administration** – for example, by reinforcing the links between various ecclesiastical communities and making them "more effective", thereby allowing local churches to "intensify [their] communion." Such an approach "favours a more intense and immediate exchange among local Churches."[25] Engagement with the digital universe will also allow the Church to "hear more clearly the voice of public opinion", thereby allowing her to "deepen her dialogue with the contemporary world."[26]

- **Deepening in faith through prayer and formation** – digital applications can "facilitate the sharing of spiritual and liturgical resources" like church-finding aids, Mass time indicators, easy access to the Holy Scriptures, online faith networks, etc.

- **Contribution to the cultivation and sharing of knowledge** – by helping to "guarantee the primary good of access to information," and by "ensuring the free circulation of ideas," digital applications and cyberspace can be "vehicles for reciprocal knowledge" or for "growth in mutual knowledge" and they have played a "decisive part" in the "spread of literacy and socialisation, as well as the development of democracy."[27]

- **Providing help in answering existential questions** – the wise use of the internet can "contribute to the satisfaction of the desire for meaning, truth and unity which remain the most profound aspirations of each human being."[28] One possible reading of the phenomenon of widespread use of digital devices is that it is a "modern manifestation...of the basic and enduring propensity of humans to reach beyond themselves and to seek communion with others."[29] Christian teaching suggests that "presenting the truth about humanity constitutes the highest vocation of social communication."[30]

2c. Threats the Church sees
from the digital revolution

- **Noise, or lack of silence** – digital communications technologies can never replace the written or spoken word, or the silent word that is expressed through prayer or sympathetic physical gestures, as they "do not favour that delicate exchange which takes place between mind and mind, between heart and heart, and which should characterise any communication at the service of solidarity and love."[31] Constantly being bombarded by electronic stimuli makes it that much harder to discern human or moral situations, as the "gentle voice of reason can be overwhelmed by the din of excessive information".[32] Pope Benedict reminds us that God spoke to the prophet Elijah not in the form of a storm or an earthquake or fire, but in a "still, small voice."[33] This makes it virtually impossible for us to "distinguish what is important from what is insignificant or secondary." According to Pope Benedict XVI, silence is an "integral part of communication," since, without it, "words rich in content cannot exist."[34]

- **Manipulation of the mind and corruption of the soul** – the absence of appropriate governance and control mechanisms, and the absence of proper formation can lead to these new media "manipulating and heavily conditioning, rather than serving people."[35] Such manipulation can arise from any number of factors including "ideologies, …the desire for profit or for power, …by rivalries and conflicts between individuals and groups, and also because of human weakness and social troubles."[36] Pope Francis cautions us that in with the internet, we inevitably will find "false coins, dangerous illusions and traps to avoid."[37] Pope Benedict XVI has warned that digital systems can be "transformed [in such a way that they] subject…humanity to agendas dictated by the dominant interests of the day [such as when] communication is used for ideological purposes or for the aggressive advertising of consumer products."[38] Furthermore, digital media can be used to "legitimise or impose distorted views of personal, family or social life,"[39] not least by undermining an integral view of the human person through pornography and via apps that fundamentally undermine marriage and the family.

- **Evasiveness and forgetting our neighbour** – the obsession with digital devices detracts from precious time with our loved ones or with people in need, as we may act as if in a daze, distracted because "our attention is fragmented and absorbed in a world 'other' than the one in which we live."[40] There is a risk that we are "less present to those whom we encounter in everyday life."[41] And it would indeed be a sad thing if "our desire to sustain and develop online friendships were to be at the cost of our availability to engage with our families, our neighbours and those we meet in the daily reality of our places of work, education and recreation."[42] Pope Francis has made clear that the digital divide presents a real risk in an era where connectivity determines whether or not persons can participate in the economy and in the mosaic of digital communications that is rewriting the very fabric of society. Furthermore, he has highlighted on several occasions the risk that we forget to "be our neighbour's keeper" even within the digital space.

- **Source of hatred** – digital media can be a destructive weapon if used to foment discord, to perpetuate injustice, to ignite or aggravate conflicts. The digital environment is one where "it is easy for heated and divisive voices to be raised."[43]

- **Narcissism, isolation, emptiness and unhappiness** – the selfie culture and the constant entry and exit into the virtual world by users of social media lends itself to a risk of "constructing a false image of oneself, which can become a form of self-indulgence."[44] It is fair to question whether it has been "wise to allow the instruments of social communication to be exploited for indiscriminate self-promotion."[45] An obsessive desire for virtual connectedness can "isolate individuals from real social interaction while also disrupting the patterns of rest, silence and reflection that are necessary for healthy human development."[46] Fundamentally, the "virtual reality of cyberspace can never substitute for real interpersonal community."[47]

- **Constant quest for external stimulation and the disconnect from reality** – in contemporary society, freedom is often described as a "relentless search for pleasure or new experiences,"[48] but the Church is clear that this is a "condemnation not a liberation."[49]

- **Speed** – why would the Church care about the speed of communications or the speed with which new technologies are adopted? Because the acceleration of history through technological progress makes of speed or technological progress ends in and of themselves. The need for speed can be a distraction, an obsession, and the "speed with which information is communicated exceeds our capacity for reflection and judgement."[50]

2d. Christian Social Doctrine principles: application to the development, distribution and use of digital technologies

These principles can be broken down into broadly nine categories, each accompanied by a list of specific measures the Church asks the faithful to undertake. The list of the Church's teachings from which these principles are drawn can be found in the Bibliography. For the sake of brevity, each source is not individually cited.

1. Ensure that digital applications can be a facility to accelerate the march of the faithful towards heaven, rather than impede it, in such a way that they help the People of God to co-operate with [God's] plan for their salvation.

   a. The need for us to remain "spiritual[ly] alert" and to maintain "constant vigilance" as we engage with these new digital media

   b. The need for an "authentically ethical approach" to using these powerful tools

   c. The need to put various forms of media "ever more at the service of the Word"

> d. The need to ensure that priests who engage in the use of digital media are known less for their "media savvy than for their priestly heart, their closeness to Christ"
>
> e. We need to ensure that despite our digital connectivity we remain "constantly attentive to those who continue to seek".

2. Using our freedoms responsibly in such a way that we are free "from the slavery of sin" (*Rm* 6:20) and recognising that human freedoms are always paired with attendant responsibilities.

   a. The need for digital media users to be educated to exercise their freedoms with a "mature responsibility"

   b. The exercise of free will and the avoidance of (modern) forms of slavery

   c. Reminding ourselves that "freedoms [are] essential for a fully human life"

   d. We must pay attention to, curate and influence, the "quality of content" that is "put into circulation using these means".

3. Putting man at the centre, as the subject, not the object, of technological progress, such that new technologies remain at the service of the human person and not the other way around; remembering that technology is not an end unto itself.

a. Ensuring the development of appropriate controls frameworks to safeguard the "centrality and dignity of the [human] person"

b. The need to respect the "primacy of the family as the basic unit of society", its rights and "presenting all its beauty"

c. The need to recognise the vital role the family plays in the development of our cognitive faculties, including how we interact with others, as "it is in the context of the family that we first learn how to communicate"

d. Ensuring the primary role of the parents in conditioning their children's internet use is not undermined, as they have a "right and duty to ensure the prudent use of the media by training the conscience of their children to express sound and objective judgements which will then guide them in choosing or rejecting programmes available"

e. Ensuring we avoid the sharing or viewing of digital information which is "degrading of human beings, ...promote[s] hatred and violence, ...debase[s] the goodness and intimacy of human sexuality or exploit[s] the weak and vulnerable"

    f. We need to ensure that digital friendships, like true friendships, are not deemed to be ends in and of themselves, but rather that they be put "at the service of the human community"

    g. Ensuring the web does not become an "instrument which depersonalises people"

    h. Ensuring it does not "manipulate [others] emotionally".

4. Being 'authentic' i.e. having spiritual integrity, or achieving a consistency between our prayers, actions, words, thoughts and desires is more difficult in digital era and "inevitably poses questions…about the authenticity of one's being".

    a. We need to ensure that as in the natural world, our interactions in the virtual world are done "with integrity and honesty".

5. Undertaking "attentive discernment", which is necessary in order to develop and maintain an "ordered use" of these new technologies.

    a. Ensuring we engage with these technologies in a "wise and balanced way"

    b. Ensuring the contents of media programmes will be "respectful of the moral law and rich in human and Christian values"

c. The need to use communication technologies in a "competent and appropriate way, shaped by sound theological insights".

6. Expressing solidarity and avoiding a "throwaway culture" as regards in particular the vulnerable, the poor, the marginalised and the weak, from the unborn to the dying.

   a. The need to ensure digital technologies are used to promote "greater respect for human rights" and "greater universal justice"

   b. The need to ensure that the benefits of digital are "put at the service of all human individuals and communities, especially those who are most disadvantaged and vulnerable"

   c. The need to create an "authentic culture of encounter" in cyberspace

   d. The need to ensure that different forms of communications media are "destined for all humanity" as opposed to being the preserve of a privileged few

   e. The need to ensure that "co-responsible participation" in the digital sphere extends beyond bridging the digital divide to include joint administration and management of these new technologies, so that a privileged few do not get to unilaterally set the agenda

    f. Ensuring it does not allow "those who are powerful to monopolise the opinions of others".

7. Supporting the full development of human potential, ensuring persons can exploit their talents, contribute materially to improving the world, discover their vocation, including their ultimate vocation as a son or daughter of God to journey towards eternal life.

    a. The need to ensure that when circumstances warrant it, communications media can "guarantee an adequate confidentiality"

    b. The need for us to ensure that in the digital era we can develop and maintain a personal environment, a "kind of ecosystem, …a just equilibrium between silence, words, images and data"

    c. The need to ensure a "healthy development for all individuals and peoples".

8. Ensuring the primacy of "direct human relations" over computer-assisted communications, as the former will "always remain fundamental for the transmission of the faith".

    a. Ensuring that those engaging in digital communications do so in a spirit of "respect, dialogue and friendship"

    b. Ensuring the media remain a "network facilitating communication, communion and co-operation"

9. Engaging in dialogue with the modern world.

   a. The need for pastors to encourage engagement with these new technologies "with pastoral prudence and wisdom"

   b. The need for those with talents in the digital arena to dialogue with the developers, distributors, operators and end-users of IT platforms

   c. The importance of engaging with the world of communications via many different mediums, and not limiting it strictly to digital (e.g. newspapers, radio, print media)

   d. The realisation that mass media "constitute[s] a patrimony" that we must "safeguard and promote"

   e. The need to have a "healthy critical capacity" with regards to the "persuasive force of the communications media".

3. Action: How can the Christian Social Doctrine guide the laity to help them engage with technology companies and inform the public debate?

Using Pope St John Paul II's call for us to (1) form ourselves, (2) participate in – as opposed to withdraw from – the challenges of our times and (3) dialogue with the world, we would like to propose a few suggestions towards becoming more informed, engaged, responsible, courageous and holy actors in the digital era.

1. Make known the Church's (relatively unknown outside specialist circles) teachings on technology and digital technology. We hope this paper can make a substantial contribution to that effort, but we recognise that there isn't to our knowledge a readily accessible, easy to digest guide on the Church's teachings on digital technology, transhumanism, and the like.

2. Enter into a more active and effective dialogue as a Church with Silicon Valley and the technology companies that are driving wholesale changes to our culture and personal habits (e.g. Amazon, Google, Facebook). We need to enter into a dialogue with

them and expose them to the message of the Christian Social Doctrine with regard to digital technology, so that they will hopefully be swayed by some of the unquestionably sound ethical principles underpinning it, and at least some of which they will hopefully apply to their business practices in the development, distribution, curation and operation of digital devices, platforms and networks. Given their lobbying efforts to shorten the working week to stem the expected flood of job displacement by automation, a good starting point might be to sensitise them to the theological value of work. As Christians, we don't only work to earn a living. Work, from a Christian perspective, has the dual purpose of allowing persons to express themselves productively, to develop their talents and their human potential but it also has the redemptive character of struggle, of achieving through effort, not because man can save himself through his own toil, but because following the fall of Adam, work can contribute to redeeming qualities in humankind. Pointing software development companies to the damage certain apps are causing to the fundamental cell of society, the family – and in some cases, naming and shaming them, if it is evident they have no interest in anchoring the profit motive with moral principles – is an absolute priority.

3. Recognise the importance of an intense prayer life, and commit to cultivating it through regular spiritual exercises, as it is "thanks to the Redemption" that the "communicative capacity of believers is healed and renewed" and the "Eucharistic encounter" is the most perfect form of communication, the moment at which communication becomes "full communion."[51] And ultimately, digital technology is a communication problem that must be solved. The breadth and scale of some of the challenges awaiting humanity in the twenty first century are such that despite our efforts, many of them will only be resolved through prayer and personal sanctity.

4. More active political engagement to sensitise our elected officials to the stakes of some of the technological developments described herein, particularly the dangerous consequences of unbridled experimentation with artificial intelligence and insufficient regulatory control over the activities of the transhumanist movement.

5. Requesting clearer pastoral guidance on what constitutes an "ordered use" of these new digital technologies – apart from just the notion of avoiding of sin or occasions of sin.

6. Developing methods for a wholesale digital detox, not by operating new-age fitness camps but through a rediscovery of the faith and more active community participation, whether religious, volunteer-based, political, athletic or cultural. Contributing to the regaining of a general sense of wonder, of divine mystery through the liturgy, and regaining contact with the natural, physical world after being overly consumed by the digital-virtual worlds by drawing upon the many positive facets of monastic life: regular schedules, simple and natural food, manual work, regular contact with nature, etc.

7. Rediscovery of silence, which Pope Benedict XVI has characterised as a "privileged state"[52] recognised as such by other religions and the rediscovery of the virtues, many of which we would no longer be able to name, by reading the *Catechism of the Catholic Church*, forming our minds; and practising virtue. In a fast-paced digital era, the virtue of patience is probably one of the most vulnerable. Our whole salvific history is a story of waiting. We say at each Mass during the Communion Rite: "as we wait in joyful hope for the coming of our Saviour Jesus Christ". And patience is intrinsically linked to the theological virtue of hope.

Bibliography of sources drawn from
the Christian Social Doctrine

Messages from the Holy Father for World Communications Day

Message of His Holiness Pope John Paul II for the 24th World Communications Day, *The Christian Message in a Computer Culture*, 27th May 1990

Message of His Holiness Pope John Paul II for the 35th World Communications Day, *Preach from the Housetops: The Gospel in the Age of Global Communication*, 27th May 2001

Message of His Holiness Pope Benedict XVI for the 40th World Communications Day, *Media: A Network for Communication, Communion and Co-operation*, 28th May 2006

Message of His Holiness Pope Benedict XVI for the 41st World Communications Day, *Children and the Media: A Challenge for Education*, 20th May 2007

Message of His Holiness Pope Benedict XVI for the 42nd World Communications Day, *The Media: At the Crossroads between Self-Promotion and Service. Searching for the Truth in Order to Share it with Others*, 4th May 2008

Message of His Holiness Pope Benedict XVI for the 43rd World Communications Day, *New Technologies, New Relationships. Promoting a Culture of Respect, Dialogue and Friendship*, 24th May 2009

Message of His Holiness Pope Benedict XVI for the 44th World Communications Day, *The Priest and Pastoral Ministry in a Digital World: New Media at the Service of the Word*, 16th May 2010

Message of His Holiness Pope Benedict XVI for the 45th World Communications Day, *Truth, Proclamation and Authenticity in the Digital Age*, 5th June 2011

Message of His Holiness Pope Benedict XVI for the 46th World Communications Day, *Silence and Word: Path of Evangelisation*, 20th May 2012

Message of His Holiness Pope Benedict XVI for the 47th World Communications Day, *Social Networks: Portals of Truth and Faith*; *New Spaces for Evangelisation*, 12th May 2013

Message of His Holiness Pope Francis for the 48th World Communications Day, *Communication at the Service of an Authentic Culture of Encounter*, 1st June 2014

Message of His Holiness Pope Francis for the 49th World Communications Day, *Communicating the Family: A Privileged Place of Encounter with the Gift of Love*, 23rd January 2015

Message of His Holiness Pope Francis for the 50th World Communications Day, *Communication and Mercy: A Fruitful Encounter*, 24th January 2016

Magisterial texts and various pastoral messages

Apostolic Letter *The Rapid Development* of Pope John Paul II to those responsible for Social Communications, 24th January 2005

Address of Pope Francis to Participants in the Plenary Assembly of the Pontifical Council for the Laity, 7th December 2013

Homily of His Eminence Joseph Cardinal Ratzinger, Dean of the College of Cardinals at the Mass "Pro Eligendo Romano Pontifice", 18th April 2005

Pastoral Constitution on the Church in the Modern World *Gaudium et Spes*, promulgated by His Holiness Pope Paul VI, 7th December 1965

Encyclical Letter *Spe Salvi*, Pope Benedict XVI, 30th November 2007

Encyclical Letter *Miranda Prorsus*, On Motion Pictures, Radio and Television, Pope Pius XII, 8th September 1957

Decree on the Media of Social Communications *Inter Mirifica*, Promulgated by His Holiness Pope Paul VI, 4th December 1963

Encyclical Letter *Redemptor Hominis*, Pope John Paul II, 4th March 1979

Pastoral Constitution on the Church in the Modern World, *Gaudium et Spes*, promulgated by His Holiness Pope Paul VI, 7th December 1965

Pastoral Instruction *Communio et Progressio,* written on the order of the Second Vatican Council, 23rd May 1971

Apostolic Exhortation *Evangelii Nuntiandi*, Pope Paul VI, 8th December 1975

Texts produced by various Pontifical Councils

Ethics in Communications, Pontifical Council for Social Communications, 4th June 2000, World Communications Day, Jubilee of Journalists

Toward a Pastoral Approach to Culture, Pontifical Council for Culture, 23rd May 1999

Pornography and Violence in the Communications Media: A Pastoral *Response*, Pontifical Council for Social Communications, 7th May 1989

The Church and the Internet, Pontifical Council for Social Communications, 22nd February 2002

Compendium of the Christian Social Doctrine, Pontifical Council for Justice and Peace, 2004

Other resources

The Power of Silence Against the Dictatorship of Noise by Robert Cardinal Sarah with Nicolas Diat, Ignatius Press, San Francisco, 2016

Endnotes

[1] Apostolic Letter *The Rapid Development* of the Holy Father John Paul II to those responsible for Social Communications, 24th January 2005, p.2.

[2] Message of Pope Benedict XVI for the 43rd World Communications Day, *New Technologies, New Relationships. Promoting a Culture of Respect, Dialogue and Friendship*, 24th May 2009, p.3.

[3] *Ethics in Communications*, Pontifical Council for Social Communications, 4th June 2000, World Communications Day, Jubilee of Journalists, paragraph cluster 2.

[4] Message of Pope Benedict XVI for the 47th World Communications Day, *Social Networks: Portals of Truth and Faith*; *New Spaces for Evangelisation*, 12th May 2013, p.1.

[5] Message of Pope Benedict XVI for the 46th World Communications Day, *Silence and Word: Path of Evangelisation*, 20th May 2012, p.1.

[6] Pastoral Constitution on the Church in the Modern World *Gaudium et Spes*, promulgated by His Holiness Pope Paul VI, 7th December 1965, paragraph cluster 4.

[7] Message of Pope Francis for the 50th World Communications Day, *Communication and Mercy: A Fruitful Encounter*, 24th January 2016, p.2.

[8] Message of Pope John Paul II for the 24th World Communications Day, *The Christian Message in a Computer Culture*, 27th May 1990, p.2.

[9] "Any purely intra-worldly ideology of progress [is] contrary to the integral truth of the human person and to God's plan in history" *Compendium of the Christian Social Doctrine*, p.48.

[10] Message of Pope Francis for the 50th World Communications Day, *Communication and Mercy: A Fruitful Encounter*, 24th January 2016, p.3.

[11] Message of Pope Francis for the 48th World Communications Day, *Communication at the Service of an Authentic Culture of Encounter*, 1st June 2014, p.3.

[12] Message of Pope John Paul II for the 24th World Communications Day, *The Christian Message in a Computer Culture*, 27th May 1990, p.1.

[13] *Ethics in Communications*, Pontifical Council for Social Communications, p.1.

[14] Encyclical Letter *Redemptor Hominis*, His Holiness Pope John Paul II, 4th March 1979, para. cluster 15, p.18.

[15] Address of Pope Francis to Participants in the Plenary Assembly of the Pontifical Council for the Laity, 7th December 2013, p.2.

[16] Message of Pope John Paul II for the 35th World Communications Day, *Preach from the Housetops: The Gospel in the Age of Global Communication*, 27th May 2001, p.2. In a slight variation on the same theme in the same speech, he speaks of the "unique opportunities [afforded by the media] for proclaiming the saving truth of Christ to the whole human family," p.2.

[17] Address of Pope Francis to Participants in the Plenary Assembly of the Pontifical Council for the Laity, 7th December 2013, p.2.

[18] Message of Pope Benedict XVI for the 44th World Communications Day, *The Priest and Pastoral Ministry in a Digital World: New Media at the Service of the Word*, 16th May 2010, p.3.

[19] Address of Pope Francis to Participants in the Plenary Assembly of the Pontifical Council for the Laity, 7th December 2013, p.2.

[20] Apostolic Exhortation *Evangelii Nuntiandi*, Pope Paul VI, 8th December 1975, para. 45.

[21] Apostolic Letter *The Rapid Development* of the Holy Father John Paul II to those responsible for Social Communications, 24th January 2005, p.1.

[22] Message of Pope Francis for the 48th World Communications Day, *Communication at the Service of an Authentic Culture of Encounter*, 1st June 2014, p.1.

[23] Pastoral Instruction *Communio et Progressio*, written on the order of the Second Vatican Council, 23rd May 1971, paras 181 and 182.

[24] Address of Pope Francis to Participants in the Plenary Assembly of the Pontifical Council for the Laity, 7th December 2013, p.2.

[25] Apostolic Letter *The Rapid Development* of the Holy Father John Paul II to those responsible for Social Communications, 24th January 2005, p.3.

[26] Message of Pope John Paul II for the 24th World Communications Day, *The Christian Message in a Computer Culture*, 27th May 1990, p.2.

[27] Message of Pope Benedict XVI for the 42nd World Communications Day, *The Media: At the Crossroads between Self-Promotion and Service. Searching for the Truth in Order to Share it with Others*, 4th May 2008, p.1.

[28] Message of Pope Benedict XVI for the 45th World Communications Day, *Truth, Proclamation and Authenticity in the Digital Age*, 5th June 2011, p.1.

[29] Message of Pope Benedict XVI for the 43rd World Communications Day, *New Technologies, New Relationships. Promoting a Culture of Respect, Dialogue and Friendship*, 24th May 2009, p.2.

[30] Message of Pope Benedict XVI for the 42nd World Communications Day, *The Media: At the Crossroads between Self-Promotion and Service. Searching for the Truth in Order to Share it with Others*, 4th May 2008, p.3.

[31] Apostolic Letter *The Rapid Development* of the Holy Father John Paul II to those responsible for Social Communications, 24th January 2005, p.7.

[32] Message of Pope Benedict XVI for the 47th World Communications Day, *Social Networks: Portals of Truth and Faith; New Spaces for Evangelisation*, 12th May 2013, p.2.

[33] Ibid., p.3.

[34] Ibid., p.1.

[35] Apostolic Letter *The Rapid Development* of the Holy Father John Paul II to those responsible for Social Communications, 24th January 2005, p.6.

[36] Ibid., p.7.

[37] Address of Pope Francis to Participants in the Plenary Assembly of the Pontifical Council for the Laity, 7th December 2013, p.2.

[38] Message of Pope Benedict XVI for the 42nd World Communications Day, *The Media: At the Crossroads between Self-Promotion and Service. Searching for the Truth in Order to Share it with Others*, 4th May 2008, p.1.

[39] Ibid., p.1.

[40] Message of Pope Benedict XVI for the 45th World Communications Day, *Truth, Proclamation and Authenticity in the Digital Age*, 5th June 2011, p.2.

[41] Ibid., p.2.

[42] Message of Pope Benedict XVI for the 43rd World Communications Day, *New Technologies, New Relationships. Promoting a Culture of Respect, Dialogue and Friendship*, 24th May 2009, p.3.

[43] Message of Pope Benedict XVI for the 47th World Communications Day, *Social Networks: Portals of Truth and Faith; New Spaces for Evangelisation*, 12th May 2013, p.3.

[44] Message of Pope Benedict XVI for the 45th World Communications Day, *Truth, Proclamation and Authenticity in the Digital Age*, 5th June 2011, p.2.

[45] Message of Pope Benedict XVI for the 42nd World Communications Day, *The Media: At the Crossroads between Self-Promotion and Service. Searching for the Truth in Order to Share it with Others*, 4th May 2008, p.1.

[46] Message of Pope Benedict XVI for the 43rd World Communications Day, *New Technologies, New Relationships. Promoting a Culture of Respect, Dialogue and Friendship*, 24th May 2009, p.3.

[47] *The Church and the Internet*, Pontifical Council for Social Communications, 22nd February 2002, p.6.

[48] Message of Pope Benedict XVI for the 41st World Communications Day, *Children and the Media: A Challenge for Education*, 20th May 2007, p.2.

[49] Ibid., p.2.

[50] Message of Pope Francis for the 48th World Communications Day, *Communication at the Service of an Authentic Culture of Encounter,* 1st June 2014, p.1.

[51] Ibid., p.3.

[52] Message of Pope Benedict XVI for the 46th World Communications Day, *Silence and Word: Path of Evangelisation,* 20th May 2012, p.2.

Has this book helped you?
Spread the word!

@CTSpublishers

/CTSpublishers

ctscatholiccompass.org

Let us know!
marketing@ctsbooks.org
+44 (0)207 640 0042

Learn, love, live your faith.
www.CTSbooks.org